Why do volcanoes erupt?

Disney BOOKS BY MAIL

DK Direct Limited
Managing Art Editor Eljay Crompton
Senior Editor Rosemary McCormick
Writer John Farndon
Illustrators The Alvin White Studios and Richard Manning
Designers Wayne Blades, Veneta Bullen, Richard Clemson,
Sarah Goodwin, Diane Klein, Sonia Whillock

Contents

What's inside the earth?

If you could dig down through the ground to the center of the earth you would find different layers of rock. The earth is like a giant peach. It has a skin on the outside, called the crust. The next layer is hot and mushy. It is called the mantle. Then there is a very hot center, called the core.

Hearing the world
Scientists have discovered what's deep inside the earth by listening to vibrations from earthquakes and movements. It's almost as if each layer of the earth makes its own sound as it moves.

Peeling the earth
The earth's crust can be up to 25 miles thick beneath the land and just three miles thick beneath the ocean. The mantle is hundreds of miles thick.

Deeply important facts

☞ One third of the surface of the earth is land. There are seven large pieces of land called continents. The other two thirds of the earth's surface is water.

☞ The temperature at the core is around 8,100°F.

Heavens above
What did the earth say to the sky?
You look heavenly today!

Why do volcanoes erupt?

Volcanoes are places where really hot material from deep inside the earth bursts or "erupts" through the surface. When a volcano erupts it throws up melted rock, red-hot cinders, and fiery gases. A volcanic eruption is kind of like opening a bottle of soda pop after shaking it. Gas bubbles in the rock froth up and squirt over the top, just like the gas bubbles in soda pop.

Lava mountains

Lava runs in streams down the side of the volcano before cooling and hardening. Often volcanoes grow into mountains from all the melted rock or "lava" that they spew out.

Look out below

One famous volcano is Mount St. Helens in Washington state. When it erupted in 1980, the top blew right off the mountain, scattering rock and ash far and wide.

Volcanic facts

☞ Did you know that there are volcanoes under the sea, too?

☞ Scientists know of 1,300 volcanoes that could erupt.

☞ In the year 79 A.D., Mount Vesuvius in Italy erupted, burying the city of Pompeii in hot ash.

How are caves made?

Caves are hollows in the ground. They can be large chambers far below the surface, or just holes in the sides of hills or cliffs. Some caves are made by rainwater trickling through cracks in the rock. Some are worn away by seawater.

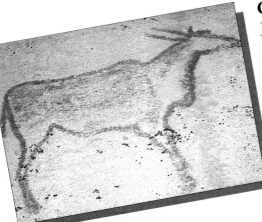

Cave paintings
Long ago, before people built homes, they lived in caves. We know that people lived in caves because they left behind beautiful paintings on the cave walls. They often painted pictures of the animals they hunted, such as buffalo and deer.

Inside a cavern
Caverns are big caves. If you could slice through a hill that has a cavern, you would see something like this.

Cave parties
What do caves wear to parties?
Stalac-tites!

Cave facts

 Exploring caves is called spelunking. People who explore caves are called spelunkers.

Caves can be as small as a cupboard, with only room for one person to squeeze in, or they can be as large as a cathedral.

How are mountains made?

Most of the world's biggest mountain ranges are crumples in the earth's surface. If you and a friend push on opposite ends of a tablecloth, you'll see how it rumples up. When the earth's surface moves, it often crumples up like the tablecloth, making mountain ranges like the Rockies and the Andes. This doesn't happen overnight though, it takes millions of years for mountains to form.

10

Feeling peaky
What do you do when you get to the top of the highest mountain?
Ev-e-rest!

Snowy peaks

These are the Canadian Rocky Mountains. High up, on mountain tops, there's lots of snow that never melts. That's because air always gets colder the higher you go.

Mountain facts

 There are four main types of mountains – fold, block, dome, and volcanic.

There are still growing, and those that formed long ago are slowly wearing away.

Many mountains are still growing, and those that formed long ago are slowly wearing away.

What are deserts?

Deserts are places where it hardly ever rains. They are so dry that only a few special plants, such as cactuses, can survive. Without plants, there is no soil – because soil is partly the remains of plants. So the ground in deserts is bare rock or even just sand, stretching away as far as the eye can see.

Hide and seek

This window plant saves water by growing in a hole underground. The only part of it exposed to the drying heat of the sun are special leaves that look like windows in the sand.

Hills made of sand

Desert sand is blown by the wind into mounds called dunes. Sometimes dunes can be hundreds of feet high.

Hot sandy facts

☞ There are fantastic rock formations in deserts such as Monument Valley, in Arizona. They are formed over many years as sand carried by the wind wears away the rock.

☞ The largest desert in the world is the Sahara in North Africa. It is 12 times bigger than the state of Texas.

13

What are canyons?

Canyons are deep, narrow valleys between cliffs of rock. They are made over thousands of years by rivers wearing their way slowly down through slabs of rock. Canyons are usually formed where rivers cut across fairly dry regions, like the Arizona desert. Eventually the rivers may dry up (or some are dammed), leaving behind an empty valley or canyon.

14

Mighty canyon
The biggest canyon of all is the Grand Canyon in Arizona. It is up to one mile deep and 200 miles long. It took the Colorado River more than two million years to wear away the rock.

Damming a canyon
By building a wall called a dam across a canyon, you can stop the river and make a big lake to supply water. Part of the flow of the Colorado River has been stopped in Nevada by the huge Hoover Dam.

Great canyon facts

☞ The Grand Canyon is from four miles wide to up to 18 miles wide at different spots.

☞ By the time the Colorado River reaches the ocean, it is no more than a trickle – about as deep as a wading pool.

What are glaciers?

Glaciers are rivers of ice that flow very slowly through mountain valleys. The ice was formed from thousands of years of unmelted snow getting packed together. It doesn't look like the ice in the freezer, though. It is full of rocks and gravel and is covered in snow.

Wooly mammoths
Thousands of years ago, there was a time we call the Ice Age. It was much colder than it is now. During this chilly time, there lived giant wooly animals called mammoths.

On the move
If you put a pile of paper on a tray, and tilt the tray, the sheets of paper slide over each other. That's the way ice in glaciers slowly moves down mountain valleys.

Ice flow facts

☞ Even the fastest glaciers move very slowly – three feet in a day!

☞ Glaciers in the Arctic and Antarctic flow into the ocean and break up into icebergs.

17

Why do earthquakes happen?

Every now and then, the huge plates of rock that make up the earth's surface move in such a way they make the ground shake. The shaking moves through the ground a little like the cars of a toy train bumping into each other when you give the engine a little shove. This shaking is called an earthquake.

Earth shakes

There are long cracks in the earth's surface called faults. In California there's a fault called the San Andreas fault. There are often earthquakes in California because the rock on either side of this fault moves.

Shaking, quaking facts

☞ Once every 30 seconds, somewhere in the world, the earth shakes just a little.

☞ Earthquakes are measured on a scale, called the Richter scale. The scale runs from 0 to 9. The higher the number on the scale, the stronger the earthquake is.

"19"

What are waves?

Waves are made when the wind blows over the ocean, moving the water and making waves. If a gentle wind blows, then the water will move a little. If the wind is strong and blustery, large waves will swirl and crash against the shore.

20

Say hello!
What does the ocean say
when it sees the shore?
Nothing, it just waves.

Salty water
Unlike river water, ocean water
is always salty. This is because it
is full of dissolved minerals, like
salt. The minerals come from
the rocks around the oceans.

Moving around
If you watch how
waves move, you will
see that they move
up and down.

High and low facts
☞ Each day, twice a day, the ocean moves
higher and lower on the shore. These
movements are called tides. When the
ocean laps further up the shore, it is called
high tide. When it drops back down
again, it is called low tide.

Why do rivers twist and turn?

As rivers run down to the sea, they wash grains of mud, sand, and gravel into bumps on the river bed called bars. Grains get added to the bars and make them bigger, and so the river has to bend around them. Eventually, the bends get so big that the river twists and turns all the way to the sea.

Horseshoe rivers

When a river flows across fairly flat, muddy land, the bends often get bigger and bigger until they are shaped like horseshoes.

Winding facts

☞ The longest rivers in the world are the river Nile in Africa, which is 4,145 miles long, and the Amazon in South America, which is 4,040 miles long.

Here today

Even the biggest lake won't be here forever. It may take many thousands of years, but eventually it will dry out like a saucer of water left in the sun, or fill up with all the mud and sand washed into it by rivers.

What are coral reefs?

Corals are tiny sea creatures that live in the shallow water of warm tropical seas, but they are nothing like fish! They are animals, but they never move. In fact, they look more like little feathery trees. When they die, their hard skeleton becomes beautiful, colorful "forests" called reefs. Coral reefs are home to millions of wonderful fish.

Ocean wonder
The biggest coral reef of all is Australia's Great Barrier Reef. It stretches for more than 1,250 miles along the northeast coast of Australia.

Magic islands
Atolls are ring-shaped coral reefs that often form in shallow water around volcanic islands. They can grow at depths of around 100 feet.

Beautiful coral facts

☞ There are two types of coral, hard and soft. Both live together in groups called colonies.

☞ There's a type of coral that looks just like a human brain – it's called brain coral.

Where does gold come from?

Gold comes from inside certain types of rock. Today, miners dig for gold in mines hundreds of feet under the ground. But sometimes, as rock is slowly worn away by wind and rain, tiny grains of gold may be washed into rivers. A hundred years ago, people got rich by panning for gold – so who knows what you might find in a river!

Veins of gold

Gold is usually found in rocks in long, thin bands, called veins. The veins were once cracks in rocks filled with water full of dissolved chemicals. Great heat and pressure turned the dissolved chemicals to gold.

Egyptian gold

People have always valued gold. One reason is because it never rusts. When archeologists (AR-kee-OL-o-jists) opened up the tomb of the ancient Egyptian king Tutankhamun, after 3,300 years, the gold mask made for him was just as shiny as new.

Shiny gold facts

People once panned for gold by collecting sand, mud, and water from a river in a large pan. They swished it all around the pan and then slowly poured out all the lighter material, and hoped that what was left in the pan were pieces of gold.

27

MICKEY'S Mind teaser

These are postcards of natural wonders. Can you remember what each picture is called?

a

b

c

d

e

f

Answers: a. mountains; b. waves; c. volcano; d. river; e. cave; f. desert.